Mother Goose
Takes a Gander at
Middle Age
A Treasury of Baby Boomer Nursery Rhymes

By Sydney Altman

Illustrated by Marty Riskin

Sydney Altman

Published by
BaBoom Press, Inc.
79 Woodchester Drive
Newton, MA 02467
Tel: 617-332-9254

Illustrations by Marty Riskin www.martyriskin.com

Graphic design by Creative Solutions, Inc. www.creativesolutns.com

ISBN: 0-9707275-0-X

Printed in Hong Kong by Kwong Fat Printing
First printing 2001

For my parents, Harry and Shavee Altman,

And to Baby Boomers everywhere.

This book belongs to:

____

Contents

Contents

Said Baby Boom Babies
It's time to take stock,

We're too young to get old
We're still rock 'n' roll jocks.

This is all a mistake,
Misconceptions must fall.

The truth is middle age
Is the best age of all.

Have you seen
the Lipo man,
the suction man,
the surgeon man?

Have you seen
the Lipo man
who works on
Sunset Lane?

Yes I've seen
the Lipo man,
he suctioned my can,
It's now flat as a pan.

I can highly recommend
the Lipo man
who works on
Sunset Lane.

This baby boomer plays the market,

This baby boomer sells by phone,

This baby boomer drills and fills teeth

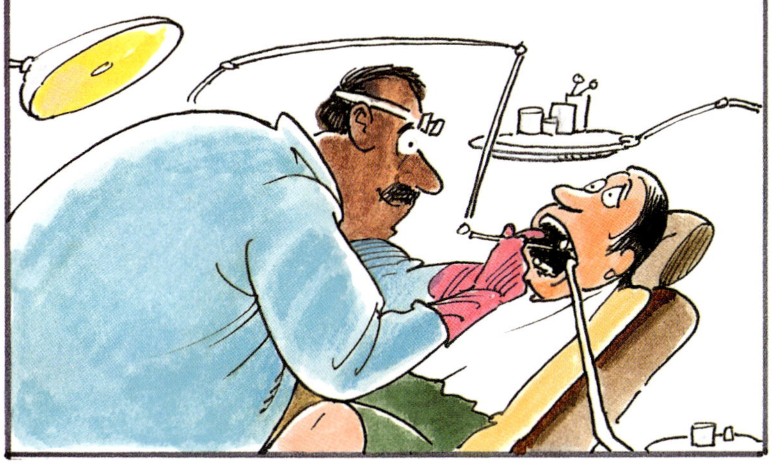

... and this baby boomer works
at home.

But this baby boomer,
Still a child of the Sixties,
Grows weed in his geodesic dome.

Jack tried to be nimble.
He tried to be quick.

He shot hoops with young guys
And ruptured a disc.

Oh where, Oh where
has my estrogen gone?
Oh where, oh where
can it be?

I was once young and fair
Now I sprout facial hair
Oh hormones please
come back to me.

Wrinkle, wrinkle there you are,
My face these days leaves my mouth ajar.

I think I used to believe that I
Was much too young to ever die.

Wrinkle, wrinkle there you are,
Old age doesn't seem so far.

He got a divorce.
He showed no remorse
He married his young thing
As a matter of course.

He put rings on her fingers.
She painted her toes.
His ex has the kids,
You know how that goes.

Ms. Peep spent a heap
Her beauty to keep
Her skin she did tuck and hem.

Leave your money alone
So you'll look like a crone:
Rich old women attract younger men.

Hippity, Dippity, Rock,
I camped out at Woodstock.
But the songs now in style
Are exceedingly vile,
I am in a complete state of shock.

Tinkle, tinkle in a jar
Yearly check-up here you are.

My LDL is much too high
I'm sure my pressure's reached the sky.

Why's his finger up so far?
I wish I'd never left my car.

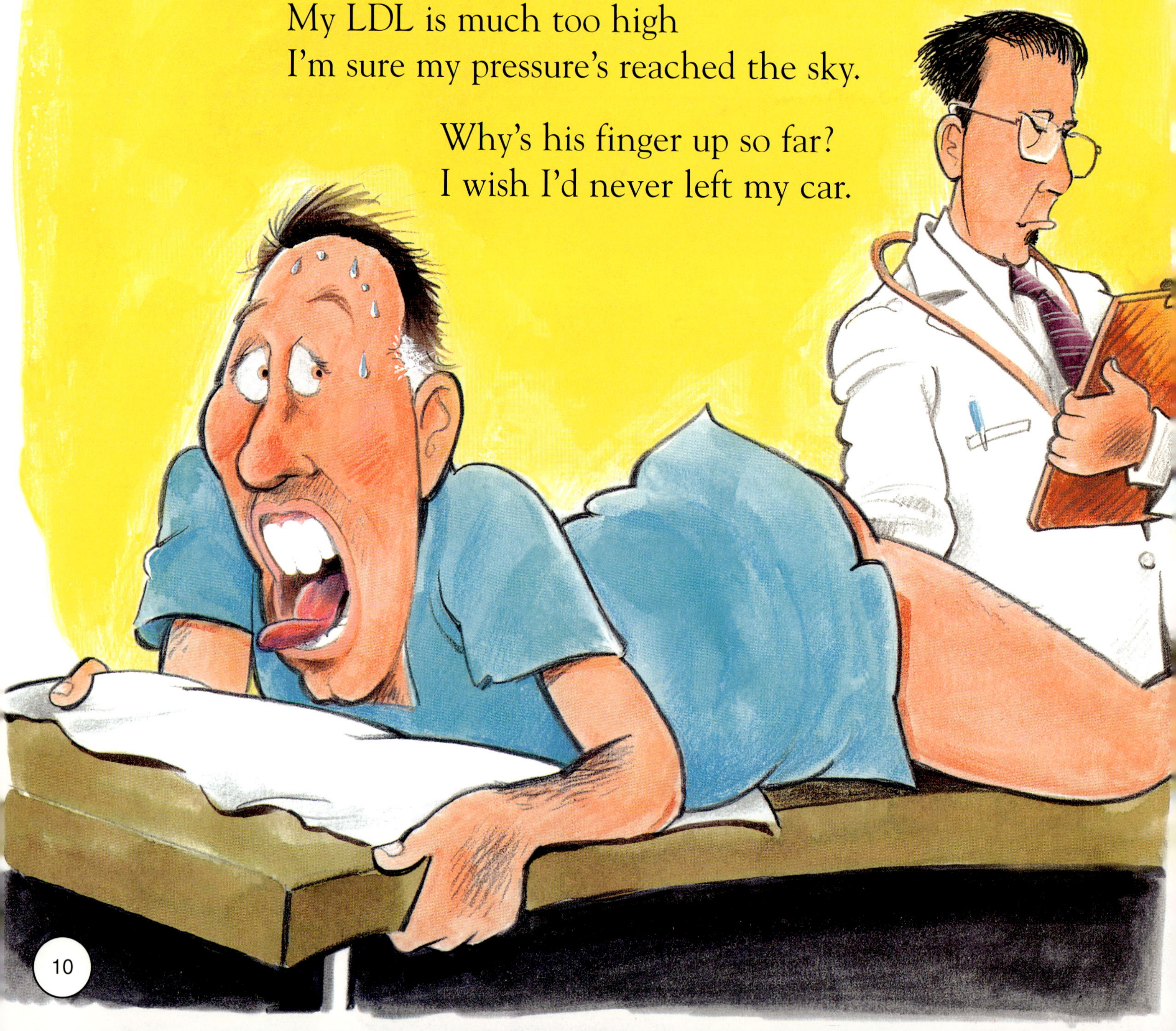

Jack and Jill
Jogged up the hill,
Their breath came
faster and faster.

Before the top
They made a stop,
Narrowly averting
a myocardial disaster.

Mr. Simon was a thigh man
Now he's in despair.
No more pats and winks at work,
Harassment's in the air.

Said in-house counsel to Mr. Simon,
"Lawsuits we can't have any."
Said Mr. Simon to the lawyer,
"I was only being friendly."

Low-fat cake, no-cal shake
Pritikin man,
I've tried every diet
From here to Japan.

I've poached it, I've steamed it,
I've drunk herbal tea.
I think from now on
I'll just let myself be.

Middle-aged Molly
on the rock climbing wall,
Prayed to herself that she
wouldn't just fall.

"I took up this sport to be
supple and fit,
But frankly, at my age,
I'd just as soon sit."

Mr. Jack Horner
Stood on the corner,
Watching the young girls go by.

When he was younger
He had sexual hunger,
Now he just feasts with his eyes.

We're the post-war generation,
A bulge within our nation.

So do as you're told,
Don't tell us we're old.

I tried to boot up,
My mouse I did click,
But learning computers
Is making me sick.

Men these days lead
such merry lives
For they can have
so many wives.

Ding Dong Bell,
My hearing's shot to hell.
I'm no longer thin,
Don't know what's out or in.

I now hold books far out
To read what they're about.
I bulge in places I was flat
What am I to make of that?

That age has done my body harm,
But hasn't stolen all my charm.

REJECTED
DENIALS
HEARTLESS
MANAGED CARE
PLAN
We Manage to be Heartless.

I do not like thee managed care,
For now I know I've not a prayer
Of getting the treatment that I need
No matter how I beg or plead.

By phone, I'm told by this stupid man,
"That isn't covered by your plan."
He suggests that I pay out-of-pocket.
Does he want me to take my house and hock it?

HMOs it's you I loathe.
Have you ever heard of the Hippocratic Oath?
Don't you know that providers are supposed to care?
Whatever happened to Dr. Kildare?

Rita, Rita, Prozac Eater,
had a friend
and couldn't keep her.

My friend, she said,
disdains all pills,
while I know they're
the cure
for society's ills.

Middle-aged Mervin
Went to the surgeon
To affix to his scalp some new hair.

But when he awoke
He looked worse than a joke
And he wished that he'd left
his head bare.

If wishes were horses I'd take a long ride,
Away from demands that tug at my side.
I'd ride long and hard
And I would ride steady,
And wouldn't come home
Until good and ready.

I once was such a leftist guy,
There was no cause I didn't try.
Joined SDS, burned my draft card,
Tried to blow up Harvard Yard.

Maturity has cleared my sight,
I now see things in a different light.
I understand that laws are good,
They protect my funds and my neighborhood.

I vote for conservative candidates
And refuse to engage in political debates.

A middle age riddle:
I now often piddle
And my figure resembles a spoon.

Yet I still have a yen
For sex now and then,
But it's young girls who make
the men swoon.

I'll tell you another:
I've turned into my mother,
Something I swore not to do.

It's very unnerving
To get dressed in the morning
And see your mom staring right back at you.

THE LITTLE TURTLE'S ADVENTURE

An
aged primipara
On a reproductive spree:
Three kids under six
At age forty three.

She fed them
and changed them
And kept them well read,
And by seven at night
They put her to bed.

Oh damn it, Oh blast it!
I've lost my reading glasses.
I left them here a minute ago,
So how come I can't find them?

Can't find them, can't find them,
Can't read a thing without them.
It's bad enough I'm going blind,
Do I also have to lose my mind?

A buyer, a shopper,
A label name-dropper,
What makes you feel like heaven?

Dot-com, dot-com,
It's changed my life
I now shop 24/7.

Mary had a lot of lamb
A lot of spam, a little ham,
Mary had two pints of jam
Her spirits were so low,
And every time she felt depressed
To the fridge she'd go.

She's joined Weight Snatchers,
And she knows
She's breaking every rule.
She dreads next weigh-in
With her gain
She'll feel like such a fool.

A man name of Morty
When just over forty
Questioned the meaning of life.

Clad just in pajamas
Went to the Bahamas,
Leaving his children and wife.

Faxes, Voice and E-mail
through the Internet I sail.
Communication's now a wonder
though it's torn my world asunder.

I still remember when I'd go
to the mailbox ... it was slow.
But I'd whistle while I ambled,
and my brain, it felt less scrambled.

Pussy cat, pussy cat
How I would preen,
When I was young
The catcalls were obscene.

Now that I'm older
No one is there,
Wherever I go
I get nary a stare.

I wrinkle, I crinkle
I no longer twinkle,
How did this come so soon?

Just yesterday I was thirty-one
I'm fifty-four next June.

Stock market, stock market
in the sky
Please, oh please,
will you stay high.

I've gotten used
to easy cash
My wife and I have
quite a stash.

Stock market, stock market
in the sky
If you crash
my funds go bye.

My bladder's gone crazy, dear Doc,
I'm up around the clock.
Every time I fall asleep
I have to take a leak.
Do you think it's my prostate, oh Doc?

A.A.R.P.
Do you take me
for a fool?

People, when
they're fifty
Don't retire
as a rule.

For male menopause
Let's hear some applause,
It's about time that men
paid the cost.

They were feeling so smug
Now let them take some drug
To restore those hormones
they've lost.

An SUV, must get one quick,
So in the snow your wheels won't stick.

What's that you say?
Oh, you don't ski,
Just stay at home
And watch tv.

Buy one anyway, you'll have a ball,
Driving it to and from the mall.

Gen-Mart, Gen-Mart, can I buy a clone?
One of me or maybe one of someone better known.

Or maybe I should simply clone my aging dog named Firth,
I truly love him dearly and he's not long for this earth.

It's such a tough decision; which clone should I choose?
I haven't had such problems since the last time I bought shoes.

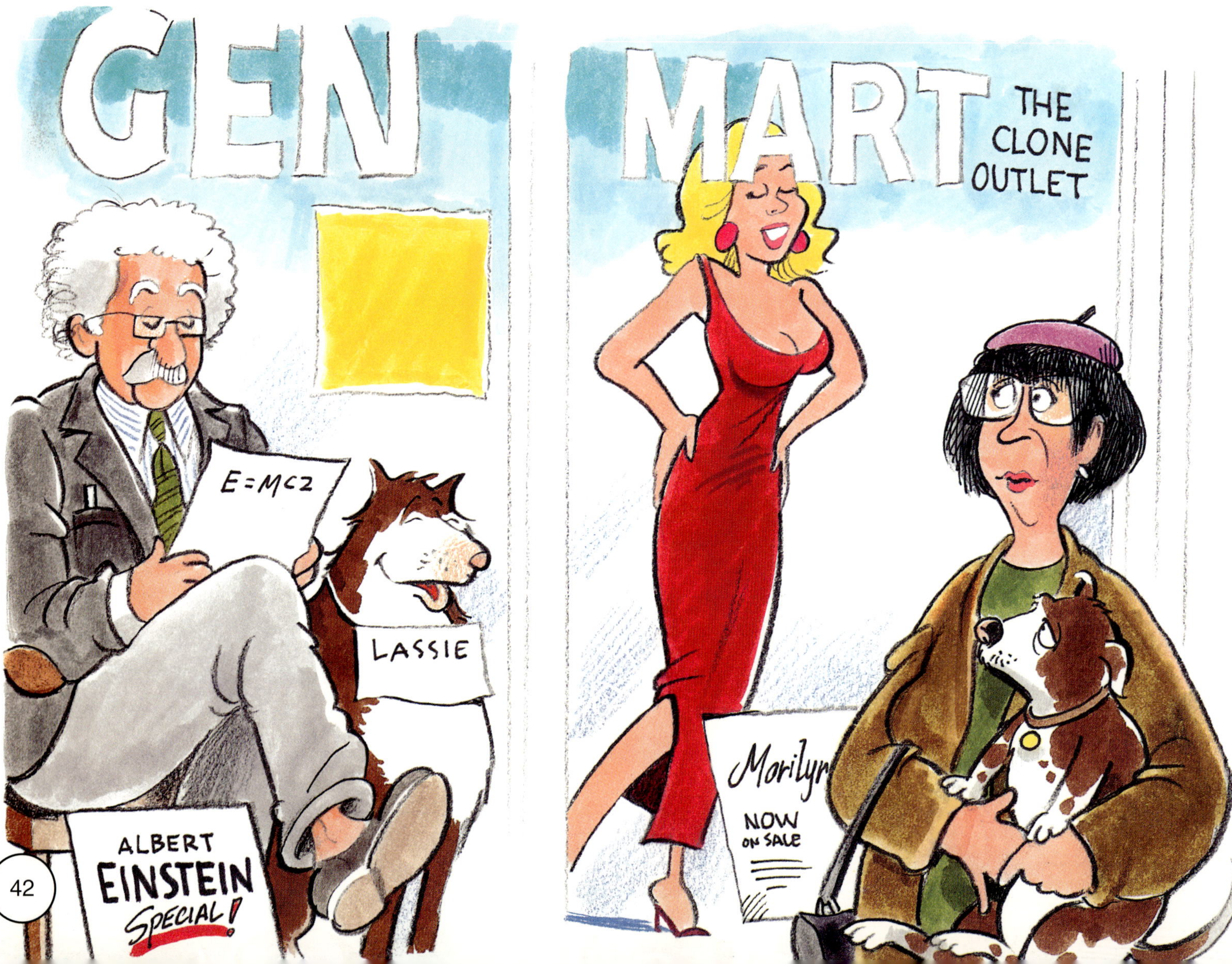

Your breasts and butt
are falling down
Falling down, falling down.
Your breasts and butt
are falling down,
My poor Sadie.

Exercise will lift them up,
lift them up, lift them up.
If you believe that bunk
you're out of luck,
My poor Sadie.

"My wife and I share equally,"
Said this guy named Cort.
"She does the house, her job, the kids
And I give her my full support."

A mild-mannered man, name of Clyde,
Went in search of his male sense of pride.
He read Robert Bly
And beat drums with some guy,
And felt he'd been took for a ride.

Osteoporosis
Please leave me alone
For I've grown attached
To my every bone.

My college reunion's coming.
I can't imagine that
It's been so long since I left school.
I can't go looking fat.

I wonder who has made it big?
And who became a mother?
I've changed my mind
Won't go at all,
I hated school,
Why bother?

I once had a tushie
So high and so round

Now that I'm older
It falls towards the ground.

APPOINTMENT
DENTIST
REMINDER
IMPORTANT
Don't Forget

I've been making no sense
My memory's gone bye.
I pause for words
It's so absurd
And here's the reason why.
Since I've started aging
My brain has lost its zing,
At the rate my cells are dying
I soon won't know a thing.

I have these conversations with my spouse,
His name is Sonny
We can't remember what we've said,
I'm glad you think it's funny.
Just because you're younger
And can still quote some good prose
Time will catch your neurons too,
By fifty they'll have froze.

Our children, our children have all left our home,
Through their empty rooms we gleefully roam.

But we fear that they'll tire of independence
And return home to us,
They hate paying those rents.

Middle-aged Stu
Go watch some porn
Your libido is shorn
Your wife is forlorn.

And where is our Stu
Who could make young girls weep?
He's under the covers,
Fast asleep.

A tosser, a shaker
A 4 A.M. waker,
What makes you wake so soon?

My midlife angst
It wakes me up,
Leaves me howling at the moon.

I once was so hip,
Even dropped LSD.
So how come my kids
Are much cooler
than me?

Investment Times
NEW STOCK OFFERING SOARS TO RECORD HIGH!

An IPO, I want one now!
I need to feed on that cash cow.
I don't want to earn money
in the ordinary way
I want to be a billionaire in just one day.

But there's a demographic quirk,
Pertaining to this shining perk.
Gen Xers hold the lion's share.
Blessed as they are with that techno flair.

While most baby boomers can just read
of cash windfalls,
Born too soon to dance at these
monetary balls.

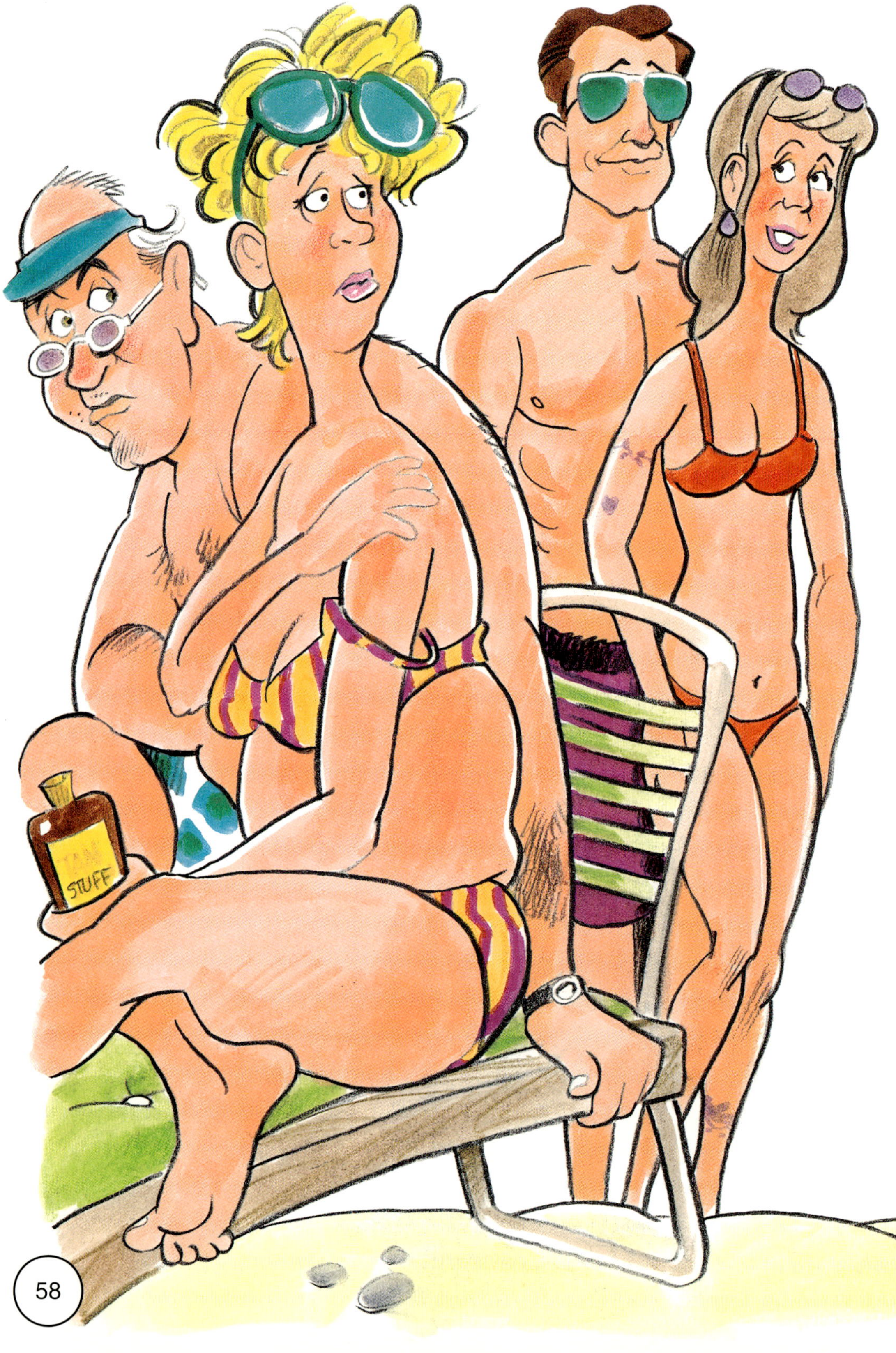

What are aging boys
made of?
What are aging boys
made of?
Love handles galore
And a proneness
to snore
That's what aging boys
are made of.

What are aging girls
made of?
What are aging girls
made of?
Addled memories
And dread thigh-
spread disease
That's what aging girls
are made of.

I'm having a mid-life crisis,
It makes me scream
and shout.

If and when
I'm young again
You'll never see me pout.

When I was young I thought that I'd
See the world before I died,
I wouldn't care which way I went
I'd live on scraps, sleep in a tent.
Now I'm older and while I'd still like to roam,
If I can't afford a good hotel I'll just stay home.

Sane Jane
let her hair go gray.

If folks don't like it
they can stay away.

Poor Mrs. Fifty
Was not feeling nifty,
Eating her low-fat Swiss cheese.

When she was twenty
She used to eat plenty
And never gained weight
round her knees.

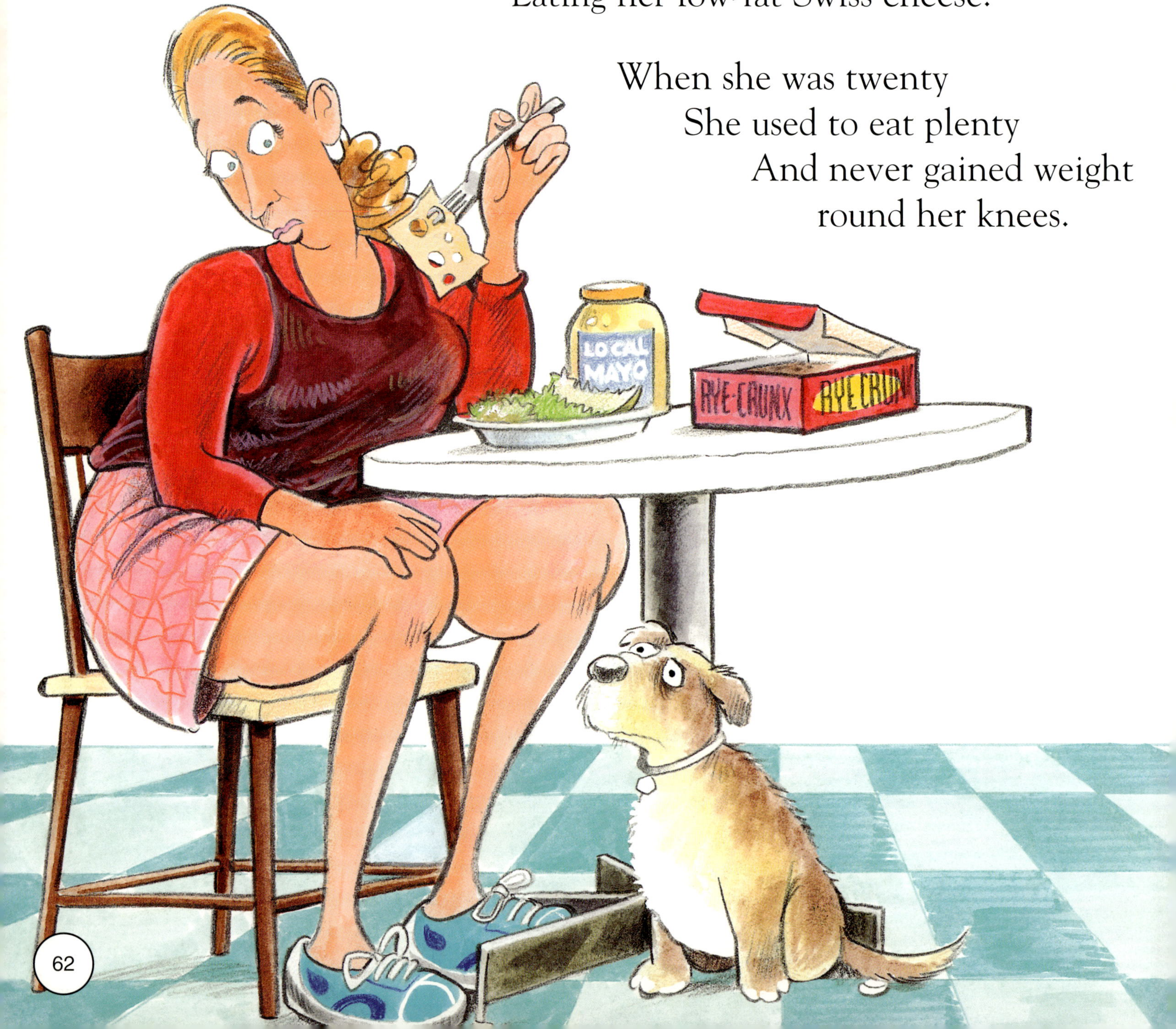

There once was a woman
Who lived in a burb:
Full-time job, Full-time kids
And a hubby named Herb.

She tried very hard
To do everything right
And frequently thought about
Hopping a flight.

Monday's child is full of face,

Tuesday's child has lost some grace,
Wednesday's child now takes things slow,
Thursday's child sometimes feels low.
Friday's child is tired of giving,
Saturday's child is rethinking her living.

But each has decided
Through a middle-aged haze
That, given the choice,
They'd like many more days.

In Case You Were Wondering …
The Original Inspirations